Living the Spiritual Laws

for Health and Abundance

Living the Spiritual Laws

for Health and Abundance

Andrew Hain and Helen W A Hain

Well Within Therapies

Published by
Well Within Therapies
26 Orchard Road
Kingston upon Thames
KT1 2QW
Telephone 020 8549 1784

Disclaimer
Every care is taken to ensure that the routines, methods and processes that are set out herein are suitable to individuals of all levels of fitness. However, please note that such material may not be suitable for all. If you have any doubts, seek medical advice prior to commencement. Cease the programme immediately should you experience any discomfort and seek medical advice.

Cover Illustration: Peaceful Shores by Andrew Hain Copyright © 1999

British Library Cataloguing-in-Publication Data
A catalogue record for this book is available from the British Library

ISBN 0-9545446-0-9

Printed and bound by Antony Rowe Ltd, Eastbourne

Contents

Introduction

Some time ago, during a difficult period in our lives, we began to search for material on the Spiritual Laws, but there did not seem to be much available that gave any insights into what the Laws might mean, or how they might be interpreted. It was almost as if the Universe didn't want us to know, or at least had decided we were not ready for this step in our development.

Gradually, though, we came into contact with the Spiritual Laws: it was as if we were being taken forwards step by step. Material became available and we read it with interest and hope. Our initial searches on the internet under "spiritual laws" produced no answers that were viable. However, when we changed the search criteria to "universal laws" we had a better response. But, good as it was, this was not the answer we required. There just seemed to be no reference book on the subject. Neither did there seem to be any guidance in incorporating their principles into daily life.

We looked for courses or workshops which might help us understand and develop, but there were none. Well, none that we could find and we did search extensively.

The message was clear. If we wanted to know more then it was down to us to do some greater research. It seems that we have been given a task to help others find their way.

Our further research produced more material, but there were differing views of just how many Spiritual Laws there are: in our searches we found anything from 10 to 105! Undaunted, we took what we believed we needed from this vast array, what we saw as the most important Laws and used them as our starting point. We believe that the 36 Laws in this book provide a good and wide enough range of ideals to live by, and will allow you to make significant spiritual progress.

We meditated on each of the Laws, asking for help from Source / Universe / God, to clarify, expand on and understand the basic statements. (We use Source / Universe / God as interchangeable terms:

you may wish to use your own term of reference.) The results of these meditative sessions appear in this book, two for each Law. Sometimes when we meditated, the channelling came through named sources, Beings of Light who wished to identify themselves. We have included their names whenever this has happened.

We would encourage you, too, to sit in the quiet and reflect on each Law, what it means to you, and record the answer in your workbook. Hopefully the contents of this book will give you some understanding of the Spiritual Laws, as well as guidance in committing yourself to living by them.

We do not suggest that what appears within this book is the only answer. However, when we went within ourselves and asked for help, this was what resulted. It struck a chord with us and we have used this guidance as a solid basis for our own commitment to living the Spiritual Laws. Take from here whatever feels right for you at this time, then develop from there: everyone has their own ways and means. We encourage you to link with your Higher Self to find your own truth.

The Spiritual Laws are there. They are given by the Universe, they are not man made. Like all Laws they are there for a purpose: to help and guide you in your Spiritual quest. We are all on earth for a reason. We all have a job to do, a purpose to fulfil. Each of us has a different purpose, fuelled by past lives and lessons. Many of us do not realise what our soul's purpose is until later in life, but once you realise what this is then the Spiritual Laws can take you forward and help you achieve it.

Our intention is that this book will be of use to group study and to individuals working alone. In trying to help you come to terms with the Laws and how best to live by them, we have posed a number of questions for you to answer, or asked you how you would react to situations. You may find it convenient to buy a **workbook** to record these answers and any notes from your meditations. We also suggest you keep a **daily journal** to record events that occur each day and your reactions to them. Using both items we believe you will find it useful to reflect on your entries and see how you are progressing.

In keeping a journal we suggest that reviews are carried out on a monthly basis. You may find it easier in the beginning to divide the journal into columns such as Date : Event : How it went / reaction : Lesson to learn (see Appendix 3).

As well as daily meditation and journal keeping, we recommend using affirmations, both of your own construction (See Appendix I) and those listed in Appendix II.

We all have difficulties in our lives. We ourselves are witness to that, particularly over the past five years. We have encountered fear, anger, anxiety, depression and serious illness to mention but a few. However we used these incidents as learning guides and, having turned to the Spiritual Laws, we came out the other side certainly wiser, but also certainly much stronger. We discovered abundance, trust and unconditional love, and our situation has changed for the better.

One last piece of advice. We believe it is no good just reading: that is passive. You have to be active. You have to BE the Laws. Live the Laws and you will experience peace, joy, abundance, spiritual enlightenment, and much more. It will not come easy, particularly in the early stages, but stay with it because the rewards are more than worthwhile.

By using the Spiritual Laws you can cut across the dogma of religion and find a code of conduct conducive to moral behaviour in any culture. Therein lies the attraction of this approach. In a sense, the early Egyptian Concept and Principles of Ma'at would seem to have a similar basis as that of the Ten Commandments and other religious moral codes, whilst the Spiritual Laws would seem to be a modern way of expressing them. As with Ma'at, and, possibly, the other moral codes, you have to live the Spiritual Laws, you have to BE them. It is not sufficient to be aware of them and use them when you feel like it. Commitment is required.

AH & HWAH

CHAPTER ONE

UNIVERSALITY

No matter how big you can imagine the Universe to be, it is bigger than that. The Universe we live in is only one of countless Universes that exist. Source is infinite. Source is everywhere. It has no beginning, it has no end. The good news is that you are very much a part of it.

We are all connected, all the seed of Source. We start this way, and we will end this way. It is only because in our physical body there is a perceived separation between Higher Self and Personality that we see ourselves standing alone. This is an illusion and it allows fear to enter the emotional body and further close the doorway to Source. However, when we experience soul growth, in some very small, but yet profound way, everyone benefits. The Universe flows through us. We are One. We are All.

Because all there is is One, all are striving for the same goal. Because all there is is One, one soul cannot exclude the growth of another.

The Law of Oneness

1. Do you find it hard to see the divinity in people who upset you? If so, why is this?
2. How can you love these people and look at the situations as separate issues?
3. In what ways are these people giving you the opportunity to learn and display your divine qualities?

No matter what interactions you have with others never lose sight of the Divine within them. Remember we are all part of the Divine, we are all one and you will then see the beauty in others. God doesn't judge us or become angry when we do something that is unloving.

We create our own situations and should be grateful for what they teach us. When others upset us we must realise we have brought this about at an unconscious level. Love the situation you have created and those who are part of it and learn from it. See only good and realise others are Divine beings on a physical journey experiencing difficult situations. Feel a connection at soul level with everyone you encounter on your pathway. Raise your consciousness above that physical problem. Look down with love and you will realise that what looked like important stumbling blocks are of no significance. Fighting situations is like fighting your shadow. Recognise the power to create that is within you and create only good.

Do not sit back waiting for things to happen.

This is a statement of the interconnectability of everything. All of God's creation is connected. You cannot bring about change to one part of creation without affecting all other parts. Certainly most of these connected changes are subtle, but they happen. You know that if you were to hurt one ankle you would still be able to walk, but you make adjustments to allow yourself to do so as comfortably as possible: so too does creation make adjustments when changes are made.

The scientist Newton understood this when he stated that every action has an equal and opposite reaction. Divine oneness ensures balance, ensures that energy is never lost. You can transmute it, but you cannot destroy it.

In the Divine Oneness we are all equal. We are all the same. Those of us who know and understand this must teach those others who do not. We must share all our talents with each other. We who understand, by our efforts, are transmuting the energy to a higher vibration and helping planetary ascension. When we all understand the whole planet will ascend, will benefit. There is no stronger number than one. For when we are one we are at our strongest point.

Applying the Law
In your workbook write down what changes you could make in order to apply this Law to your daily life. For example ... separate the person from the problem, be a better listener, do not blame others for my unhappiness.

Meditation Suggestion
Why not try a Walking Meditation? Just take yourself off to somewhere in nature -- a quiet riverbank, a forest, mountains, a country setting -- and use all your senses to get in touch with nature. Feel that you are part of it, part of all creation. Write up your experiences in your workbook.

CHAPTER TWO

CAUSE & EFFECT / KARMA

Karma is the principle of cause and effect. Every cause has an effect and every effect has a cause.

Karma is the learning tool of Source, and manifests through physical circumstances. Karma does not discriminate in its application: it affects everyone.

We should strive to ensure that actions should be seen to be "non-harming": towards self, other people and to all other living things. It means being kind, gentle, respectful and considerate towards all.

Law of Action

1. *What does it take to get you active? What processes do you go through?*
2. *In what ways do your everyday actions serve your life purpose?*
3. *Do you need to change your thinking to bring your actions and purpose into line?*

Action comes from the individual and begins with an idea, a thought which then can become reality. It is important to have the right thoughts, the right plans otherwise what you intend may never happen, may not become reality.

What is your life purpose? How can you serve? Use these thoughts and your actions will be on the right lines. Have a purpose and make it known. Talk about it, write it down, visualise it, intend it and use affirmations. This is tied in with the Law of Cause and Effect. Have the right intentions, carry them out and the effects of your actions will bring satisfaction.

Action is how you behave. It's about what you think. In the Law of Motion you are told that everything is energy. Thoughts become reality. So too does this Law reinforce that message. Thoughts become actions in reality. You act out what you think. As your thoughts are born and take root so do they grow and transmute to become actions. This is how you create your reality. Thoughts, words, actions, they are different stages of the same energy.

Actions speak louder than words. How often have you heard that? Words can be powerful, spoken or written, but actions are the manifestations of words. Doing is committing: this is why actions go beyond words. Many offer fine words, but do not carry out the actions that back up the words.

By your actions you demonstrate your reality, display who you really are. Spiritual growth comes not just through thought, not just through word, but through action as well.

Page 16

Applying the Law
Describe a difficult situation you are now facing? What action have you taken? In what ways do you need to change your thinking to achieve a positive outcome?

Law of Cause and Effect

1. Recall a negative action you took. What were the consequences and / or repercussions?
2. Recall a positive action you took. What were the consequences and / or benefits?

You have heard that for every action there is a reaction and this is true. This law doesn't just apply to actions --- it applies to thoughts as well. In fact thoughts are the forerunners of actions, so cultivate pure thoughts of love when planning your actions.

Sometimes thoughts go around in the mind and don't lead to specific actions. You may have thoughts of anger, fear, resentment in your mind. These emotions can go round and round in the mind and these negative thoughts linger within causing all manner of illness and disease.

Be in control of your thoughts. Be aware of the effects they have on you and others. You project these negative energies not only to your bodies but out to the Universe where they are picked up by others at an unconscious level. Healing thoughts bring love and healing to others so remember the effects that negative thoughts can cause.

Be in control at all times, thinking of the effects you can have on yourself and others. It's like being one step ahead. Realise the power you have to enable you to be in control. You have no need to complain when things go wrong --- they are what you have attracted. Think love, feel love and that is what you will attract.

Beloved child, Kwan Yin here. There is much in common between this Law and the Law of Correspondence. There is nothing you can think, say or do that can happen in total isolation. To everything there is a reaction, an effect. Sometimes it is equal and opposite, sometimes it starts a chain reaction. On other occasions I have given you the metaphor of the pebble and the water. [*See Law of Correspondence*] I used it to explain that everything is connected. I could easily say to you that it also applies here.

No matter how remote you may believe something is, be it an idea, a thought, a word spoken or written, or an action or deed, it will have an effect somewhere in the Universe, and even knowing that this is so, you cannot possibly know exactly where, on whom or how.

Cause and effect guide you to be careful in your thoughts and deeds, for the wrong word or the poor example can have catastrophic results. Kind thoughts and good examples, on the other hand, manifest in pleasant experiences. My child, there is not a lot more to say.

You create your own reality and you thereby involve others and affect their reality. Just as you do not like negative influences from others in your reality, so you should not cause anything but positive influences on theirs. Cause and effect occur because everything is One. Remember that and step positively into your reality.

Applying the Law
In your workbook write down what changes you could make in order to apply this Law to your daily life. For example ... see the good side of people, take others' feelings into account.

Meditation Suggestion
Think about a problem, a relationship or difficult situation.
- Send out healing, love and forgiveness.
- Visualise the situation as pleasant, amicable, etc, -- how you would like it to be.
- Bring back the good feelings and be aware of them the next time you are in the situation.
- Record the outcome of the experience in your workbook.

Living the Spiritual Laws

CHAPTER THREE

ENERGY

Energy exists in various forms. Energy can be transformed, but it cannot be created or destroyed.

Energy can also be pure thought. Energy is Source.

Law of Motion

1. Consider the ways in which you are in motion when you are still.
2. Take a few minutes break several times a day and consider the thoughts you have been thinking. What emotions did they show?

The Universe consists of nothing but energy. Our bodies and minds are energy and so too are the objects around us. Energy vibrates at different levels, hence we can see our physical bodies which vibrate slowly, but not our spiritual bodies.

Energy is in constant motion although our physical eyes are unconscious of this. Energy has its own consciousness and therefore its own abilities. It is important that we use these abilities for good as like attracts like. Loving thoughts will attract love, anger will attract anger.

We have to realise the potential within to create and to ensure we create what we really want and what is for the good of all.

Everything indeed is in motion, even those things which you perceive as not moving. Items you think are dead, have no life, are inanimate, are in motion. Your scientists have long since discovered this. The invention of the microscope and later the electron microscope showed science a world beyond the visible. At atomic levels there is much movement. Applied universally it is understandable that even in the so called vacuum of space there is movement.

Back on earth now. Take your body, it moves constantly. Even in your stillest moment you move. Your heart beats without your intervention, you breathe without noticing. Thoughts are generated, sometimes at such an alarming rate you wonder where they all came from. Thoughts then become reality, and from one state to the other there is movement.

Movement is an everyday physical phenomenon, but it has a Spiritual aspect. The earth spins round on its axis and you mark this unfelt movement with a device called time. The earth spins round the sun, and the sun, in turn, spins round a greater entity. Movement goes on forever.

You cannot stop it. So be careful with your thoughts for they can be unstoppable once created.

Applying the Law

In your workbook write down what changes you could make in order to apply this Law to your daily life. For example ... be aware that the thought process is endless, take more care of my body.

Law of Energy

1. Energy is always on the move, changing from one form to another, but never being "lost". In what ways have you altered the state of energy?

2. If you notice a negative thought cancel it and replace it with a positive one. Note in your workbook how things change for you.

I am Jayan. I know that you wish a better understanding of this law. All is energy and everyone themselves being energy has control over energy. This is brought about by thoughts and desires. Thus it is important to be aware of this and learn to control thoughts. When thoughts run riot havoc is created by these thoughts on a physical level inside and outside the body.

Slow down the thought process --- check the thoughts that run through the mind and ask if you really do want them. Think about what the consequences of them might be and be prepared to change them. Be in control of your thoughts and you control your experiences.

You are the creator of your experiences. Often you don't realise this and blame others. Realise the power you have to exercise change. Negative experiences can be transmuted by the right thoughts which lead to positive actions. Use your healing energies to transmute what seems inappropriate. Take responsibility and look for positive results.

Energy is the source of everything. Energy is everything. Every thought, every word, every deed and action. All are manifestations of energy. Your presence on earth is a collection of energies, vibrating at different levels. Your physical body is the lowest of these vibrations. Your mental, emotional and spiritual bodies, which you cannot see, vibrate at higher levels. These bodies are not separate, but are connected to each other and energy can pass from one to another.

Energy changes, or transmutes, as it moves between vibrations. That sense of well being you get is energy passing through the vibrations and having a positive effect or influence. On the other hand negativity can creep through, resulting in emotional problems, for example.

Energy by its very nature is always on the move and is therefore prone to changes. Indeed it's a fact of the Universe that energy transmutes as it moves. You influence it with your thoughts. You influence it by your attitude. As before, it's about creating your reality -- transmute the energy to how you want it to be. Some say fight fire with fire, but there's no need. Simply transmute what is wrong into what is right. For what is wrong is only energy in a different form and you can change it if you have the heart and will to do so. Energy is constantly changing. Use this for positive results.

Applying the Law
In your workbook write down what changes you could make in order to apply this Law to your daily life. For example ... take responsibility for my thoughts, turn negatives into positives.

Law of Rhythm

1. What rhythms do you go through in your everyday living?
2. What changes can you observe in Nature that are important to human life?

Everything is energy vibrating at different rates but there is always rhythm and perfect timing in natural laws. The tides come and go with amazing accuracy, the phases of the moon, the rising and setting of the sun can tell you the time and date.

Your physical body too has incredible rhythm --- the cells die and reproduce, your metabolism slows down and speeds up with night and day. The seasons come and go bringing change to the environment. Nature is successful due to the inherent rhythm which man cannot destroy. He tries to control this and seems to be partially successful but only for a limited time as nature will change rhythm and fight back successfully.

You can fight the rhythm in your body -- lack of sleep, poor diet, negative emotions and all seems fine for a time but unless the body is allowed to find its own balance illhealth and death will result. Take time to observe your own body rhythms. Listen to what your body is saying and find balance in all aspects of living.

Take time to listen and observe the flow in nature. Be in tune with nature and allow your rhythm and the rhythm in nature to be in harmony together.

The Law of Rhythm concerns all things. To everything there is a rhythm. Your life is a rhythm -- you are born, you live, you die. Often you repeat this rhythm many times over hundreds of years. It is the rhythm of the soul as it moves forwards and upwards.

As you live you are caught up in all sorts of rhythms. Your heart, your life giver, beats with a rhythm that lasts as long as is required. It may beat at many different rates as you live out your life, but always with the same rhythm.

Your world spins with a rhythm that is so precise that it can be accurately measured. Its passage through the heavens and round your sun are further examples.

There is rhythm to the seasons and one will follow another with a surety that is so fundamental to life on the planet.

Plants and animals have their own rhythms, like you, but all are dependent on the planetary rhythms. Rhythm is the basis for everything and we must listen to Mother Nature's rhythm, the rhythm of the Universe, of Source.

When we are tuned into that rhythm, when we make ourselves aware of it, then truly we find peace and understanding. When we are at one with Source, with the Universe, with Nature, we are at one with ourselves. There can be no greater joy than this. Make time, take time to discover the wonder of rhythm.

Applying the Law
In your workbook write down what changes you could make in order to apply this Law to your daily life. For example ... I need to spend more time with Nature, plan and carry out an exercise pattern, listen to what my body is telling me.

Law of Attraction

1. In what ways, by using which tools / techniques, can we attract the "right" things to us?
2. Think of something you want in your life. Write an affirmation and decide on the first positive steps you can take to doing something that will help you achieve it.

Many people are unaware of the power they have to create their experiences. It is easy to blame others when things go wrong or don't turn out the way you want them to.

It is easy to apportion blame outwith yourself instead of realising the power that is within. This is why it's important to take responsibility for thoughts and actions. What is given out even as a thought will attract similar back to you. Be in control of thoughts and you control your experiences.

Negative thinking brings negative experiences and illhealth as all levels of bodies are interconnected.

People are beginning to realise this but there are still many who do not have this awareness. When circumstances are undesirable realise the power of thought can change the experience.

Attitudes and thought are of prime importance. Accept the circumstances and thank the Universe for this opportunity to grow. Send love to whatever and whoever is involved. The giving of love will bring love back to you.

Take control by being aware of your thoughts otherwise negative thoughts will lead you to giving away your power to others and the outcome may be what you were trying to avoid in the first place.

I will step forward. Djwal Kuhl. You are familiar with the concept, the idea, that thought is creative. That what begins as a thought becomes, in stages, a reality. You know therefore that you create your own reality.

Reality is how you perceive things to be. Reality is what you want things to be. Reality is how you want things to be. You create your reality by thought. You turn thoughts into visions. You turn visions into reality. In the visualisation stage you are creating. You are like an artist painting a picture. You include all the elements you want and you arrange them as you would wish. You then empower the visualisation and in doing so turn it into reality. What you are doing is magnetising your desired elements, pulling them to you. This is the attraction.

Whatever you think, whatever you visualise, you attract it to you. So, there is danger. The Universe is bountiful and will grant your requests. So you must exercise care in what it is you are asking for, and in what circumstances the request is made.

Ask and you shall be given. This is where affirmations are useful, because the process helps to eliminate the negative, and plants a positive seed from which thoughts and eventually reality are created. The Law of Attraction is there to remind you that what you think is indeed what you get. Think carefully, think wisely.

Think love and attract love. I hope these few words have been of benefit. DK.

Applying the Law
In your workbook write down what changes you could make in order to apply this Law to your daily life. For example … be more organised, write affirmations, stop dwelling on things that are outwith my control.

Law of Creativity

1. Creativity can be demonstrated in numerous different ways. What are your talents? (Even your journal and workbook are unique, as they have been created by you. They are an expression of what is within you.)
2. How often do you display these talents?
3. In what ways have you changed since keeping a journal?
4. Is there a relationship / situation you have been responsible for improving / empowering?

Everyone has their own potential to create. All is part of God the Creator and hence creativity is an innate quality. It is part of each person's uniqueness. Creativity can be displayed in many ways.

Not everyone takes the time to discover their true gifts, their true potential. Taking time to work with one's Higher Self allows inspiration to flow through. By using talents and abilities one serves others and can fulfil one's life purpose.

Share your skills and bring beauty into the world. Remember creativity isn't just about using skills, it's about using the power within to create your reality and experiences. Pay attention to your thoughts and feelings.

Remember how powerful these are and that whatever you focus on will be attracted to you. Creativity isn't just about producing beauty. It can bring about what you want to avoid.

It is important to have pure thoughts, think positively and trust that everything has a positive outcome. Take responsibility for your outlook and actions and what you attract will be what you really wanted to create for yourself and others.

Creativity is such a powerful, positive force. It can be applied to so many things. Creativity starts with a thought, an idea, an inspiration, and manifests its way through to being. It is like the reality we each create by the thoughts we give birth to and feed until fruition.

Creativity is not the talent of the gifted. Each and every one is creative. We create each day, each moment. Our creativity never stops, not even when we are asleep.

Creativity is not necessarily an art thing either. Many devices and everyday objects are taken for granted, but someone created them. Creativity can mean looking at old ideas in new ways, bringing new wisdom to old philosophies. There is no end to creativity, and if you believe in your creativity you change your reality. It would be against man's spiritual nature not to create, not to change reality.

There is now a growing acknowledgement of this and so, as more accept their co-creativeness, the planet evolves. Creativity is a positive powerful force. Harness it and use it constructively.

Applying the Law
In your workbook write down what changes you could make in order to apply this Law to your daily life. For example ... take time each day to use as many talents as possible, be open to change and take risks.

Meditation Suggestion
Get yourself into a comfortable, relaxed position. Place both hands, palm down, on your body just below your ribs and be aware of your abdomen rising as you breathe in and falling as you breathe out. Keep your attention on your breathing. As thoughts come into your mind -- and they will -- just acknowledge them and bring your attention back to your breathing. At the end of your meditation make a note in your workbook of the thoughts that you had during this session. This will give you an insight into what your mind is concerned with.

CHAPTER FOUR

RESPONSIBILITY

Each of us is, without any shadow of a doubt, responsible for every thought, word, deed, intent, motive and action.

Once we establish the boundaries of our responsibility we can take full charge of that which is our duty, and let go of that which is not. By doing so we will find enjoyment in supporting others as we create more harmonious relationships. By establishing the limits of our responsibility we can avoid becoming over-involved in other people's lives.

Law of Honesty

1. What are the consequences of not being honest with yourself? Do you gain anything by taking this view?
2. Keeping your journal will assist you in being honest with yourself. Are there aspects of your life that keep reappearing in your journal?
3. In what ways can you take more responsibility for your actions and thoughts?

If you really love yourself you will be honest with yourself. This is a step you must take before you can love and be honest with others. Continually examine your thoughts and actions to make sure they are in tune with what you really want to believe. It is all too easy to go along believing yourself to be acting in a spiritual way when, in fact, you are not.

It is easy to blame others instead of taking responsibility for yourself. Take time to stop and look below the surface. Look for ways to make your actions more loving and raise up your consciousness. Ask for guidance before rushing into things and it will be easier to be honest with yourself. You will not have regrets or feel bad about how you've reacted.

Be continually looking at your own shortcomings. By being patient and understanding with yourself you will become more understanding and loving towards others. You will be aware that everyone is on his or her own pathway and that no one is perfect. Do your best and realise that others are doing their best also.

This Law is about being true to yourself first, and then to others. Your Higher Self knows what is true -- listen to it. Let your conscience guide you, for it is the signpost of the Higher Self. Do not betray yourself for that will lead to dilemma and conflict -- to pain and self recrimination.

Do not fear what your conscience tells you: it will not harm you. Neither deny what you know, deep inside, to be true. You can fool your ego, but you cannot hide from your conscience. It is true that sometimes the truth hurts, but that only happens when you have tried to shut it out.

You must always be true to yourself. When you have learned this, then you can be true to others. Living a life of truth will keep you on your spiritual pathway, and will keep you on target to meet the objectives your Higher Self set when you were born.

In life we may drift from our goals, targets and path through our denial, through forgetting or ignoring the truth. We should evaluate each day and ensure that we are living according to our conscience, to our Higher Self. If we are not then our journey is going nowhere.

Applying the Law
In your workbook write down what changes you could make in order to apply this Law to your daily life. For example ... be more honest with myself, review my journal with someone else on a regular basis.

Law of Responsibility

1. In what circumstances are you responsible for others' actions?
2. Describe a time when you blamed someone else when you should have taken responsibility.
3. How do you feel about the idea that by taking responsibility for your thoughts and deeds you control your reality?

You must take responsibility for all your thoughts and deeds. No one else can do this for you. Do not blame others when things go wrong. Be observant of yourself at all times. Mindful of self is vital to staying in tune with the Higher Realms.

Check all thoughts, words and deeds at all times and change them if they do not fit your interpretation of the Spiritual Laws. This is taking responsibility for your life and no growth can take place if you don't observe. Observation and analysis will lead to improvement and success.

Make all that you do a meditation and you will be aware of yourself on all levels. To avoid responsibility leads to being dishonest with yourself and in turn being dishonest with others. Being responsible is being in control and having awareness of self.

For some, responsibility is like a weight they do not want to carry and they offload it to others. However we are not responsible for another's burden, only our own, and so, someone who does not want to carry their responsibility only thinks it is being carried by others.

In truth the responsibility remains with them. The denial of responsibility only masks it: it does not get rid of it and one day it has to be faced squarely. Better to accept that you are responsible for all your actions, deeds, thoughts, words, attitude -- everything you think, do or say. That way you can control what is happening and can direct your energies according to your needs and plans.

Your Higher Self will direct you on this, for it knows where you should be going along your spiritual pathway. If ever in doubt about anything seek out the silence and go within.

You have a responsibility for your spiritual journey -- a responsibility to see it through to its end. You have a responsibility to be positive about your life and its fulfilment. Your Higher Self entered into an agreement with Source and you have a responsibility to ensure that the agreement is kept. You must therefore do all you can to achieve the spiritual goals set by your Higher Self.

Applying the Law
In your workbook write down what changes you could make in order to apply this Law to your daily life. For example ... do not be afraid, admit when I have been wrong.

Meditation Suggestion
Review your journal. What qualities do you need more of? In your meditation breathe in each of these qualities in turn and note what it feels like to have them. Record this in your workbook.

CHAPTER FIVE

PURPOSE

Without purpose we are nothing. We will do nothing, we will achieve nothing. Purpose gives meaning.

Law of Aspiration

1. Do you always give of your best? If not why not?
2. What are your ambitions? How will you achieve them?

By linking up frequently with your Higher Self you will realise the potential within you to be a being of love and light. Do not lose sight of this connection to the Higher Realms. This connection will constantly remind you of the right thoughts and the right actions you need, no matter what the circumstances.

There will always be times when you are in a physical body that you will be surrounded by people who present negative feelings and circumstances. By connecting upward to your true self you will be guided towards the right feelings and actions. You will be reminded to send love to these people and events instead of being drawn into negativity and returning like with like.

You will be able to turn events around in a loving way. By raising your own vibrations you will also be raising the vibrations around you. This is exercising your full potential and bringing Heaven to Earth. Change yourself and you are also changing the world around you.

In all aspects of your life you should be aspiring to the highest. To do one's best in all activities, to give of one's best at every turn. To be a leader is the way of the spiritual warrior. To be an example for others to follow. To show strength, to be purposeful. Be an inspiration for others. Be positive, be caring, be sharing, be loving, be joyous.

Life may seem complex, but life is simple. Keep it simple and love it to the full. Let your simplicity be joyous. You have an abundance so share it. Help those who are struggling to simplify their lives. In simplicity there is much to behold. Strive for simplicity and you will achieve the higher potential.

Applying the Law

In your workbook write down what changes you could make in order to apply this Law to your daily life. For example … having a more determined attitude, giving from the heart.

Law of Courage

1. What is courage? Where does it come from?
2. What qualities do you need to enable you to show courage? How can you develop more courage?

The spiritual path is not the easy option. It takes courage to remain focussed on where you are going and courage to continually examine your progress.

Keeping a journal and noting your events and reactions each day is well worth it. You may not like what the truth is but with courage to continually monitor yourself you will see progress.

Look to your Higher Self and Beings of Light who are there to assist you and you will stay on the right path. It is easy to fall by the wayside and lapse into ways which don't demand much effort. Nothing worthwhile is easy. Have the courage to look inside at your true self.

Have the courage to stand up for your beliefs and what you know to be true. There are many battles to be fought as you go through life but the hardest battle is against your own ego. Have the courage to say 'no', the courage to be honest and true to yourself and your path will become easier to follow.

———————

Courage. Be strong. Be positive. Trust, and all will be well. There is always guidance available, even in your darkest moments. The light never deserts you. Go within. Seek out the quiet and go within.

Never lose touch with your Higher Self. Your Higher Self will guide you. Trust the feelings. Trust the judgment it makes. Your Higher Self is connected to the Source at all times. From Source you came, to Source you will return. To Source you are always connected. Source cannot, will not desert you.

Therefore, in your moments of doubt, in your times of despair, use the connection. Talk to your Higher Self. Listen. Trust. Act. Always try to

maintain a positive outlook. It's not a case of putting on a brave face --
it's a case of believing in Source. That will give you courage to face the
bad times. Courage to pass through the experiences successfully.
Courage to learn, to adapt, to grow.

Never fear, we, in the Higher Realms, are always with you. We are here,
not to protect you as such, but to guide you, to work with your Higher
Self, to give you the courage to walk your path.

Applying the Law
In your workbook write down what changes you could make in order to
apply this Law to your daily life. For example ... be willing to take
risks, be honest with myself and others.

Law of Dedication

1. Does dedication to something mean you cannot change?
2. What qualities would help you to be dedicated to what you believe in? What hinders your dedication and causes you to lose motivation?

It is important to give your whole self to what you believe to be right and true. Do not go into activities or missions half heartedly as the enthusiasm will soon wane with little achieved.

Check out your feelings at all times and trust your intuition. If it feels right go for it and give it your all. Go forth in life with a purpose. Remember you incarnated with work to do. Serve Source in whatever way feels right. Do not become rigid in your ideas. Remember that as you grow you will find different aspects of truth.

Be open to new ideas and knowledge but stay firm on your path. Whatever work you do, do it with love and remember to show love to others, even to those who may not approve of what you are doing. Trust your intuition, ask for guidance and be committed to whatever you put your energies into.

To be dedicated to a person or cause means that you believe in them or in it. You are committed to them, to it. You believe in them, in it. You are giving of yourself in your dedication. This is good if you truly believe, if you totally trust, and deep down it is what you want to do and believe to be true.

However do not dedicate yourself to anyone or anything blindly. There can be many factors to consider and this you should do. Weigh up what dedication will mean to you, how it will affect you.

Always look inwards. Consult your feelings, your Higher Self. If it is right then you will know, and you can plan accordingly. In your dedication you must always review and, if necessary, change targets, change views, change goals. Keep your objectives in focus.

Other people, other events, other things all interact with your views and beliefs and you should review, challenge, adjust according to your feelings. What is right for the Higher Self is right for you. Trust your Higher Self, it won't let you down.

Applying the Law
In your workbook write down what changes you could make in order to apply this Law to your daily life. For example ... remain focussed on what I want to achieve, meditate more to get further ideas.

Law of Leadership

1. When the going gets tough the tough get going, so they say. Do you always stand up to be counted? What stops you?
2. How willing are you to share your Spiritual beliefs with others?
3. Is it only like minded people you share with? If so, why?
4. To what extent do your actions demonstrate your beliefs?

Whatever you have been given is for sharing with others. This includes all the knowledge and wisdom within you. Do not force your beliefs on others but be willing to share with those who desire to know more.

You have acquired knowledge from others who have shared their truths with you. You have learned much from books and by observing others. Be willing to offer what you have in service to humanity.

Live what you believe to be true. Do not say one thing and do another. Share your beliefs and experiences in a truthful way but not a dogmatic way. Never be afraid to state what you know to be true. This is being honest with yourself and others.

Leaders have to be trusted. Maintain an open mind and be flexible in your belief system. Never be afraid to state your ideas and beliefs but know that these may change as you progress.

Encourage others to take in whatever knowledge is available to them but allow them the privilege of assimilating this and accepting what is right for them or rejecting what is not. Be a leader not a dictator.

Sometimes you have to stand up and be counted, as it were. There are times when saying nothing causes more harm than good. There are times when it needs to be said. To make your position clear, to define who you are and where you are coming from you have to take the lead and be prepared to set the example.

There is enough of moral judgment going on. It is actions that demonstrate your commitment. Leading by example, from the front, shows you are fearless, shows you have belief. In everyone's life there comes a point when enough is enough and they will spring into action.

Your day for this should be every day. There is no need for crusade, for you are not out to convert or win battles. You are demonstrating who you are and where you are going. Others may follow, but they are not your responsibility. You have to do this for yourself. In a sense this is selfish, but you are only responsible for your own actions and beliefs.

If you believe then do it. If you are committed be it. Have no doubts, be forthright. Do it, be it. Now.

Applying the Law
In your workbook write down what changes you could make in order to apply this Law to your daily life. For example … share knowledge, be less willing to suffer in silence.

Meditation Suggestion
Ask your Higher Self to show you your purpose in life and how you can be of service. Your Higher Self has a gift for you to assist you on your Spiritual journey. Accept this gift with thanks and note the nature of the gift. Record this in your workbook afterwards.

CHAPTER SIX

LOVE

Love is a warm emotion we are all capable of feeling and expressing. Some perceive being loving as a sign of softness or weakness. However it takes tremendous courage to express love when you really feel and mean it. Each and every one of us, without exception, has a responsibility to act with love in every thought, word, deed, intent, motive and action.

Law of Self Love

1. List 10 things you like about yourself.
2. How easy was it to do this?
3. Choose someone who has hurt or upset you and make a list of their positive qualities.

The Law of Unconditional Love does not mean just applying this to others. You yourself are included in this. Love yourself on all levels. By all means strive to progress but do not become angry and unloving towards yourself when you feel you have failed.

Learn from whatever lessons come your way and honour the progress you make as a result of them. Take care of yourself on all levels to maintain health. This shows you care about yourself and love yourself. Remember the saying 'as within so without'. This care and love will be visible to others and you will be able to radiate love to all around you.

Be understanding and tolerant with yourself and you will extend these qualities to others. It is not selfish to love yourself and care for yourself as this is the first step towards loving others. You have to experience these qualities in order to share them. Love yourself and it will be easy to love others.

You chose this body. You chose this personality. Because you exerted your free will you have a duty to love who you are. Previously we have said everyone has their responsibility to carry.

In upholding your responsibility for what you say, think and do, so too should you love who you are. When you love who you are then the steps along the path towards your goals become easier. You will gain in confidence and you will plan your activities with the right attitude and in the right frame of mind.

Do not let anyone deflect you from loving yourself. This is easier said than done, especially when the criticism comes from those you respect and trust. This is not to say that all criticism you receive is bad, criticism is only acceptable when it is constructive and reasoned.

Don't be afraid to reject any criticism you receive so long as you take time to understand what is being said.

Feel the joy of self love, feel the freedom to satisfy your needs and wants.

Express yourself in a positive manner. In doing so take care to ensure that you are not putting others down. There is no gain in doing something at another's expense. What you do is for the good of your Self, not your ego.

Applying the Law
In your workbook write down what changes you could make in order to apply this Law to your daily life. For example … forgiving self and not feeling guilty, have more confidence in my own abilities.

Law of Unconditional Love

1. What causes you to make demands, judgments and expectations of another?
2. This is a difficult Law to live by, but it is important that you do so. Make a list of people you find it difficult to love and your reasons for this. Are you demanding certain ways of behaviour (eg love in return)?
3. How would you feel about writing in your journal that you would prefer certain actions from others but that it won't affect your love for them if they do not change? If you can do this, well done. If you can't, love yourself and your less positive aspects and you will gradually find it easier to accept others.

This law encompasses all the other laws. If you can show unconditional love at all times you will be observing the other laws as well. You will love others without expecting love or anything else in return. You will not lay down conditions, behaviour or emotions on their part.

You will truly be on the right path with no fear. Love conquers all. If you give out love only love will return so you will have no problems with the Law of Cause and Effect. Love yourself and take responsibility for yourself, leaving others to have freedom of choice. The love you give out will protect you from any negative thoughts from others.

To maintain unconditional love you must be aware of all your thoughts, words and actions. If they are not of love change them and you will notice that even in difficult situations all will be well. You are the creator of your reality. Use love as the building bricks and your world will never collapse around you.

Unconditional love is the greatest gift you can give or receive. It means you do not judge and are not judged. It means acceptance of others for what they are -- a fellow spiritual being walking their pathway.

It means not placing pressures on anyone to perform or conform to some synthetic standard. It means you are open, honest and completely trustworthy, not least with yourself. It means making no demands and creating no expectations.

With unconditional love you will never be disappointed because of all these things. When you receive unconditional love all these things apply to you -- no demands, no judgments, no expectations. In summary you are free when you give out and receive unconditional love. Whatever you do, whatever you say, whatever may be your beliefs, temper them with unconditional love and note how you are rewarded. As you give so shall you receive.

Give out unconditional love: the rewards are great. Freedom, hope, honesty, trust, joy, fearlessness, selflessness. These are just a few. There are many more waiting. Love. Unconditionally.

Applying the Law
In your workbook write down what changes you could make in order to apply this Law to your daily life. For example … accept others as Spiritual Beings, let go of critical thoughts, be patient and understanding.

Law of Free Will

1. When was the last time you did something "against your better judgment"? What were the consequences? How did you perform? How did you feel?
2. How do you react to the idea that you always have a choice?
3. Free will enables you to create your own reality. Do you find this a wonderful challenge or a responsibility you'd rather not have?
4. The free will others have provides us with opportunities to grow and learn. Do you agree / disagree with this statement?

You may feel at times that you have no free will, that circumstances are put in front of you and you have no choice as to how you react. Remember you have chosen to experience certain events and circumstances for your spiritual growth.

You have free will as to how you will react. The lessons to be learned are there but you have to use your free will in the best way to learn and grow. You always have a choice as to how you react. We say always choose a reaction that displays love, love for those involved and love for the opportunity to learn and progress.

Free will is a huge responsibility. Using it in a selfish way causes hurt to others, not to mention how it affects you. What you do and how you react will have repercussions. Take responsibility seriously. Realise what can be created by your attitudes and decisions.

Use your free will wisely and for the highest good of everyone involved. Free will is a gift from your Creator so endeavour to make sure you use it as a gift to others. Remember others have free will also, so respect whatever choices they make.

Free will is every human being's right. We are all born with it. We do not lose it, but some decide to give theirs away. They do this through fear, through lack of self esteem. They do this by allowing others to take control of their thoughts, deeds and actions. By doing so a person ceases to "be".

Free will allows a person to express who they are. It is the medium through which each of us relates to all others. It allows a person to live in the moment, to go with the flow, to be spontaneous. Free will is the essence of life.

When one expresses and uses free will there is much vitality, much joy. Take it away and you subdue, bring darkness, hopelessness. Free will is yours. Reclaim it if you have to. Use it. Express it. See the happiness it brings. As you discover more and more who you are so too will you express your free will.

Without free will you do not live. You exist at a low level. Raise your vibration, raise your spirit. Release your free will and express yourself to the full.

Applying the Law
In your workbook write down what changes you could make in order to apply this Law to your daily life. For example ... be more assertive, do not make demands, be willing to make decisions to change aspects of my life.

Meditation Suggestion
- Surround yourself with people you find hard to love.
- Breathe in love with every breath, filling every cell in your body with love.
- Then allow love to flow from your heart to the heart of each individual in turn.

(Some people "see" Love as a colour during meditation. If you are one such person then breathe in that colour then send it out to the individual with whom you wish to build a better relationship.)

CHAPTER SEVEN

TRUST

Assurance (promise), belief (true or real), confidence (intimacy), expectation (looking forward to), faith (loyalty, belief in something without proof), hope (something desired), reliance (dependence on) ….
What does Trust mean to you?

Law of Faith

1. List some recent events you consider to be a coincidence. What happened afterwards? Was it coincidence?
2. Can you see a connection between events in your life? For example one job led to something better but you needed that experience to get to where you wanted to go. Can this help you see current situations in a different light?

This law encourages you to look beyond the surface of events and circumstances of your life. Know there is a purpose in all things and trust that the purpose is for your spiritual progression.

Do not complain or become despondent when things do not go the way you would like. Remember you chose the circumstances of your life before birth and these were chosen for particular reasons.

Accept what comes your way and look at how each day can bring new growth. Look at how events in your life work out and how often one thing has led onto something else. If you become anxious and fearful and complain you will be attracting even more difficulties with the negative vibrations you send out. You will sink deeper into despair.

Be calm and ask for guidance. Be patient and go with the flow. Believe that you will be taken care of. Love every situation and be grateful for what it has to offer you.

Have faith, put your trust in the Universe. You will be looked after. The Universe provides abundance -- you have to realise this. Source provides what is needed, when it is needed, in the amount it is needed. This is abundance.

Everything that happens does so because it needs to happen at that precise moment. Some see this as a phenomenon called coincidence. In reality it is the Divine Plan in operation.

Whatever has occurred has a relevance for you, and you should examine it. Always there is something for you -- you shouldn't have to doubt it. I don't mean you shouldn't examine the circumstances, but you should never doubt that there's something in it.

Always, without fail, there is something for you. Always there are lessons or opportunities. The Law of Faith says that you know this to be true and that you will seek out the knowledge. Knowledge is power. It is your power to determine how you will progress. Never give up on the chance to gain knowledge, be empowered, and take control of your life. Trust. Have faith.

Applying the Law
In your workbook write down what changes you could make in order to apply this Law to your daily life. For example … go with events patiently, know that changes will come at the right time, look for connections.

Law of Hope

1. What are your hopes and fears? How will you achieve one and avoid the other?
2. What makes you feel pessimistic / optimistic?
3. The next time you feel you are losing hope what steps could you take to get on course again?

Hope is an inward knowing that all is well and all will continue to be well. To experience this it is important to be in tune with your Higher Self, seeking guidance and staying firmly on your spiritual pathway. You know that each step along the way is progress.

If you lose contact with Source and your Higher Self it is difficult to trust when things do not seem to go in your favour. You sink into despair and the negative thoughts you send out attract even more negative vibrations towards you, keeping you in a vicious circle.

Be steadfast on your path and in your thoughts. Know that energy is in motion and nothing remains the same.

Look forward to each new day and give thanks for what it brings. Know that you are never alone. Hope for the best and your positive outlook and faith will take you through all situations.

By remaining positive you will be a support for others who feel there is no hope of surmounting their difficulties.

It is said that where there is life there is hope, but it is also true to say that where there is hope there is life. Hope is the womb of progression. When all else fails, hope will build anew.

Hope is believing there is a better way. When trouble is all around hope will pull you through. Hope is being positive. Hope is seeing the good side of any situation. Without hope there is nothing.

Hope is what you build your future on. Hope is what you base your reality on. Hope becomes your journey along the pathway and keeps you going through the storms. Hope is the rainbow. Hope is the silver lining. Hope is the future.

Be strong. Have faith in the Universe. Hope will guide you for it is your beacon in the darkness. Your hopes become your thoughts: your thoughts become your ideas; and your ideas become your reality. Fear not. Despair not. Hope will not abandon you. Hope is your strength.

Applying the Law
In your workbook write down what changes you could make in order to apply this Law to your daily life. For example … do not allow negative thoughts to be dominant, never give up, do not be pessimistic.

Law of Joy

1. How do you express joy? Do you sing? Dance? Jump up and down? Do you keep it to yourself?
2. When you feel joyful what are you telling the world and those around you?

Most people experience happiness but they do not know the meaning of joy. Happiness can relate to everyday physical experiences and is often at a superficial level.

Those who desire to follow their spiritual pathway find happiness at a deeper level and this is pure joy. It is deep within one's being when one opens one's heart to the Higher Realms.

When you have found joy you have also found peace and an inner knowing that everything works out in the right way for all concerned. Trust that you will always have your needs met and this will enable you to let go of fear and attachments.

This brings the experience of peace and joy within your heart. Happiness can be a fleeting experience but joy comes when you are connected to your Higher Self and it is not something others can give you.

Joy is a wondrous feeling. A feeling of excitement, a feeling of fulfilment. A knowledge that you found that which you were seeking, an expression of well being. So spontaneous is joy in its expression that you release great energy to the Universe.

Joy is an expression of unconditional love. This is how life should be at all times. How to keep this feeling with you always? Know that there is a purpose and a reason to all things.

Each event in your life, each encounter you make, each coincidence has its purpose. Look for the purpose and learn. Look for the reason and grow spiritually. Do not worry. Do not despair.

Do not entertain gloom and despondency. These will depress you, these will suppress you. Look for the positive. Seek to be impressed, look to express.

Express your joy in any way that you can -- sing, shout, laugh, smile, inspire, encourage.

However you do it, tell the world. A joy shared is a joy doubled. Let that positive energy flow through and round the Universe. Joy unbounded. Let that be your goal.

Applying the Law
In your workbook write down what changes you could make in order to apply this Law to your daily life. For example ... go with the flow and look for the positive in each experience, know that everything is as it should be, realise there is much to be joyful about.

Meditation Suggestion
Put on a favourite piece of music that uplifts you. Relax and close your eyes and be aware of the feelings that you experience. Record them in your workbook. You may want to use different pieces of music each time you do this.

CHAPTER EIGHT

GIVING & RECEIVING

Thanksgiving: thanking people for their contributions and thanking Source for the blessings we experience during the day.

Forgiveness: when we realise that people act and react because of their particular personality types, we can stop taking their behaviour personally and are able to truly forgive them.

Sharing: giving of ourselves: giving time, attention, effort, knowledge, talent and love.

Offering: giving up an attachment. This could mean we give money, a pair of shoes, a garden tool or anything that has value for us.

Law of Compensation

1. What are the differences between inducement and compensation?
2. How do you react when you are given something? Do you think you deserve it?

Whatever you have is a gift from the Universe -- be it money, talents, love, skills. You have been provided with these and they are not to be kept and used selfishly. Give of them freely as they were given to you.

Do not judge others --- give unconditionally from the heart and you will experience abundance as the gifts you have given return tenfold. Whatever you have is energy which must move and not stagnate. If it does then no one gains, least of all yourself. Be willing to accept gifts as well as give and be grateful for whatever is given. Remember to give to yourself. A healthy body and mind are essential to serve others.

Knowledge is a gift and is also for sharing. Time set aside for helping others or sending healing is also rewarded. Each day when you look back at how it has gone, as well as giving thanks consider how much you have given away. Whatever you have has been given for a reason and should be used appropriately. Be open to both giving and receiving.

My friend you have asked for guidance and I have been asked to bring it to you. My name does not matter, it is the message that should interest you.

The Law of Compensation ensures that you will be rewarded for each good thought, word and deed. It is the encouragement you need to act and think appropriately.

However it is not bribery, for that is an inducement to do something you don't want to do. No, the Law of Compensation is in the background, it is low in profile. Indeed you really needn't know it's there at all. When you have given from the heart, out of love, you have given of yourself. Spirit compensates this act of love by rewarding you spiritually. Who can place a value on seeing a smile? However, you grow spiritually.

All those things that you regard as being priceless, these are the compensations for giving of yourself. You are aware of when you have been compensated, and in this awareness is the knowledge that you have done or said something for all the right reasons.

You certainly don't get this when you do something because you think it is how you are expected to react. When you give from the heart you do so unquestioningly and because you do so the Universe recognises your unselfishness and your reward, not that you looked for one, is all the greater.

Applying the Law
In your workbook write down what changes you could make in order to apply this Law to your daily life. For example … appreciate the efforts of the giver, be spontaneous in giving.

Law of Charity

1. When was the last time you gave to charity? What did you give? Why? How did you feel?
2. Be willing to share talents, gifts, money, etc in a non-judgmental way with those in need. Is there something you could do or give today that would show you demonstrating this Law?

Remember this law in order to keep energy flowing freely. Whatever you have in life is a gift and is for sharing with others. Give freely from the heart and you will never be without.

Give where there is a need and give with unconditional love. Do not judge others. You never know the whole picture so you cannot say someone deserves help and someone does not. That is conditional love.

Do not withhold help in any form. Share whatever gifts you have and trust you will receive accordingly. Good comes in all kinds of guises. If you cannot recognise this how will you know where to turn when you yourself are in trouble.

Charity is looking after those less fortunate than yourself. Charity is encouraging, nurturing the vital energy. Charity is doing everything to ensure that it grows and manifests.

Charity is being positive. Charity is loving unconditionally. Charity is helping others take responsibility for their lives. Hold yourself up as an example by loving unconditionally, by taking responsibility for yourself, by reaching for the higher potential.

Always, remain positive, see the good that is in everything. Don't let despondency creep in. It is true that every cloud has a silver lining. Through striving for the highest you will see the lining and forget the cloud. When you share what you have found, what you have experienced, that is charity.

Applying the Law
In your workbook write down what changes you could make in order to apply this Law to your daily life. For example ... accept others as they are, keep an open mind, appreciate what I have and be willing to share it.

Law of Generosity

1. When was the last time you gave something away because you had more than enough for yourself? Were there any subsequent happenings?
2. What stops you from showing generosity? (fear, not having enough, judgmental)
3. In what ways have you benefited from the generosity of others?

Whatever you have is a gift from the Universe. You are custodian of these and it is your job to see that they are available to those who can benefit from them. Do not store up your possessions. This shows attachment to them. You then become fearful of losing them and it is to this end that your energies are directed. What a waste of energy.

Be loving and giving, willing to share with those in need and the Universe will return your generosity according to your need. This is abundance. As well as being generous with your material possessions such as money, be generous with your time, your loving thoughts, your knowledge and wisdom.

Do not force anything on others but make your talents available to those who seek them. Selfishness shows fear of loss. Be open to giving and receiving, knowing that your needs will be met whilst serving others.

Give from the heart, living each day at a time with no fear for the future.

We all can afford to be generous -- in our praise, in our help, in our endeavours, in our commitment. On our spiritual journey we should not hold back or count up the cost. If it is worth doing, it is worth doing wholeheartedly.

Generosity is a recognition of abundance -- what you don't require for yourself give to others. Strive to be abundant, strive to be generous. These two ideals go hand in hand. Has it not been said that "as you give so shall you receive"?

Greed, wanting more than you need or can use, is selfish and egocentric. Whilst you should look after yourself, this should not be done at the expense of others. We are all interdependent. We all grow because of the experiences we create for each other. No one person is more important than any other.

If we have more we should use our gift of generosity to recycle it. Everything is energy, and energy must be allowed to flow freely. Indeed it is each our duty to ensure that it does.

Generosity is giving without thinking, about giving without wanting in return. Generosity is a manifestation of unconditional love. Let it happen.

Applying the Law
In your workbook write down what changes you could make in order to apply this Law to your daily life. For example ... give away those items for which I no longer have a need eg books, clothes etc, be open in my giving -- if it is worth giving do it from the heart.

Law of Kindness

1. What was the last random act of kindness you were involved in? When? What was the outcome?
2. How do you feel when kindness is rejected?
4. Do you find it easy to accept kindness?

If you love unconditionally you will show kindness to all life with no questions asked and seeking no reward in return. Give from the heart without judgment and your kind acts will be returned to you.

Kindness can be shown in many ways and is not just about sharing worldly goods. A smile, a handshake can mean so much to another. Do not force others to accept your kindness as this is not unconditional love. Allow them their right to accept or reject whatever you offer.

Be open to giving without fear of going without yourself. Know you are abundant and you will have no problem about sharing what you have with others. Do not judge as you never know the whole picture. A kind act with no selfish intent will always be the right course of action.

————————————————

Kindness, Joy, Generosity, Giving. They are all manifestations of unconditional love. Acts of kindness are a recognition of the spirit in others. It's an energy exchange. It helps universal energy to flow more freely.

How often have you heard the saying "One good turn deserves another"? Acts of kindness encourage others to act and react in a similar way. In making an act of kindness, indeed in giving the gift of kindness, you are doing from the heart.

You are giving from your Higher Self. In doing so you are not expecting anything in return. It's the declaration of unconditional love. The doing, the being, the giving are all done because, deep inside your heart, deep inside your soul, that is the right and spiritual thing to do. Joy is yours.

There is no need for greed for it cannot buy anything that is worthwhile. There is no need for anger or resentment for it will only hold you back. There is no need to be grudging, for kindness costs you nothing materially, but great is your reward spiritually.

Neither is there any need to feel morally superior because of your kindness. This is ego making a judgment. Listen to your heart, to your soul, be kind to others and know the joy and happiness. Sharing everything you have is the way forward.

Applying the Law
In your workbook write down what changes you could make in order to apply this Law to your daily life. For example ... smile more, mean what I say and do, be cheerful and approachable.

Law of Thankfulness

1. Write a letter of thanks to God / Universe / Source and list at least 20 things for which you are thankful.
2. Think of a past difficult situation and list what you learned from it and give thanks.

Being thankful is being able to see the positive side of everything and appreciating what you are given whether this is in the form of gifts or experiences from which you can learn lessons.

Each day examine what you have received and give thanks. If you hold resentment then lessons will return until you gain something from them. Appreciate others even those who cause you upsets and problems as they are your teachers.

Count your blessings making sure you do not miss the less obvious ones. Stay centred in times of difficulty. Do not become pessimistic. Ask for assistance and guidance when you go into the quiet.

Ask what lessons are being presented if you are unsure, and, by doing this, you will be able to appreciate and say thanks for everything.

Be glad and enjoy each day as it unfolds. There are many things to celebrate. List all the things you take for granted, a whole list of items that you rarely give a thought to, but which enrich each and every day.

The Law of Thankfulness can be stated as adopting the attitude of gratitude. If you adopt this attitude, this way of thinking, this way of being, you will help move those universal energies round. You will aid your spiritual growth in so doing. You will be giving out, and receiving, the gift of unconditional love.

Never think that you know everything, never think that you are superior. Judgments are all relative and who is to say what is right for someone else. Never forget who you are and where you are going.

—

.

Always return to the silence and go inside. Your Higher Self will remind you of these things. Look around you and remember why you are here. Even in your darkest moments you should give thanks, for without the dark how do you define the light? Without misery how do you define well-being?

There is positive in everything and you should be thankful that this is so. Give thanks for everything in your life. By doing so you acknowledge its existence. This way you move along your chosen path.

Applying the Law
In your workbook write down what changes you could make in order to apply this Law to your daily life. For example ... examine each day at its end and be grateful for what it brought, never take things for granted.

Law of Abundance

1. What stops you from being abundant?
2. What are your views on the following statement? "Abundance is a state of mind".
3. Write an affirmation to use daily that will assist you in feeling abundant.

Abundance comes from trust. If you fear losing something you lose it. It goes, you can't hang on to it. Abundance is the free flowing of gifts --- you have them and you pass them on. They are there when you need them but you don't pile them up.

Your needs have always been met and will continue to be met. Give to others and let the gifts flow. Give in order to receive --- not just money but love, time, effort.

Having abundance brings contentment. Faith is required. You must be sure that everything you do fits in with your life plan. What you give out comes back --- maybe not in the same form but you will be taken care of.

You have learned to do with less and you have had all your needs met. Go with what happens and don't try to fight it off. You realise that lessons are learned and abundance comes naturally.

Keep examining your pathway. Don't fear failure, criticism or lack of needs being met.

Abundance is having what you need when you need it. Sometimes you have to plan ahead to create abundance. For example the sowing of crops in one part of the year means abundance in another part of the year. So too is it with other things.

Abundance is not wealth in a monetary sense. You can amass a fortune but not be abundant. Abundance concerns the things that matter to your growth, both physical and spiritual.

Give out: get back. If you love everything, that love will return to you. If you love joyously, joy will be returned to you. Whatever it is you want to be, give it out first, then watch as it returns to you. You have heard the saying "one good turn deserves another". This is a summary of abundance in action.

You do not need fortunes of money, gold or jewels to be abundant for they cannot buy the products that make up abundance. The simple things in life are what make up abundance, and the good news is that they are free of monetary cost.

The real cost of abundance is that you have to give of yourself. By giving of yourself you are keeping the flow of energy on the move and as it goes round it will surely return to you.

Applying the Law
In your workbook write down what changes you could make in order to apply this Law to your daily life. For example ... be in the present and do not fear, do not hoard, give a donation to the first person or charity requesting my help

Meditation Suggestion
Experience an Eating meditation!
- Sit down to a meal in silence, either alone or with a like minded friend.
- Pay attention to the taste, smell, texture, etc of the food you are eating.
- Thank the Universe for supplying you with this food and send thanks to those who have participated in the growing, harvesting, etc of it.

CHAPTER NINE

NON JUDGMENT / ACCEPTANCE

Source does not judge you: judgment is a human invention. Judgment is a means to control as we do it against an artificial and / or idealistic standard. Judge not, for if you do you, too, will be judged.

Law of Compassion

1. Do you ever think of the needs of others? What do you do about their needs? Are there simple acts or gestures you could make?
2. Think of ways you could show compassion to people you don't know. For example making a donation to charity.

You can see that all the laws revolve around one i.e. that of unconditional love. To be compassionate you need to enter the world of the other person, be aware of their needs and to convey your concern and willingness to assist.

This may involve sharing your physical possessions but a smile, a handshake, a nod can convey so much. Do not shut yourself off in your own world as you will become blind to the needs of others.

Send out your loving thoughts and healing prayers even when you do not know someone personally and even when you do not know exactly what assistance is required. The angels know what is to be done and can use your loving thoughts to bring about a healing of any situation.

If someone needs your help and you have a grudge against this person from the past release any negative energy with a white or violet light so that unconditional love can flow to them.

Compassion is unconditional love. Compassion is not pity. Compassion is expanding the passion that already exists. Making it bigger, greater, more joyous.

When you make a judgment about a person, a situation, you are diminishing that passion. You narrow the outlook, you diminish its potential. Look on all things with compassion, not judgment.

Jesus said "Judge not lest ye be judged". Indeed his message was one of unconditional love to all people and all situations. Compassion is an expression of unconditional love.

Through compassion you will find peace, you will find hope, you will find joy, you will find what it is you are seeking. Through compassion you will learn. Through compassion you will grow, and your spirit will know no bounds.

Compassion is strength, compassion is spiritual fulfilment.

Applying the Law
In your workbook write down what changes you could make in order to apply this Law to your daily life. For example ... be more aware of others' needs or difficulties, take time to get a sense of how others may feel.

Law of Acceptance

1. Do you think it is wrong to interfere with another's free will? In what circumstances would you interfere in others' actions or decision making?
2. What are your reactions when someone you love does something you disapprove of?

Very often interfering with others' choices is well meant. However this is an attempt to take away their power and their right to take decisions. This is control and denies others free choice. If they retaliate against interference this causes upset and animosity.

Resentment can linger for a long time and relationships can be destroyed as you become alienated from people you say you love. It can be painful to see others make what you consider to be mistakes and wrong decisions, but who says they are wrong? You do not know what experiences they need to grow, so do not deny them the growth which will come from each experience.

To love unconditionally means you love someone without putting down rules and regulations. If you feel someone is making a poor choice, taking risks or bad decisions you may wish to point out consequences, but, if so, do it in a loving way and be prepared for your advice to be rejected.

Love them, love their mistakes and faults if that is what you think they are. Be there to support them if they ask for help. It is better to be silent and send out loving thoughts and a healing prayer than to interfere and regret it later. Love others as they are.

You will never know all the reasoning behind their decisions and even if you did, you cannot expect them to change. Love others, set them free and do not allow your happiness to depend on their choices.

Non interference means respecting the being of all others. You do not hold responsibility for others so you must allow them to choose according to their will, not yours. By all means share with others and offer counsel, but do not impose will. Everyone is a being of free will and this must be respected.

Ask that others be wisely guided and looked after, but, at the end of it all, it must be their decision. Send unconditional love and trust that they are making the right decision according to their needs, views and beliefs.

If you treat others with the respect they should have, then you will find that you too will be accorded this freedom to do as you see fit. Non interference does not mean that you don't care or are unloving. Far from it. Non interference shows that you do care and are trusting enough to allow others to make their own decisions.

You are responsible only for your own pathway. You have a job to do to be sure that you are achieving your own goals. In reality you do not have time to get involved in another's journey.

As I have said before give help when asked, counsel wisely when called upon, but resist with great strength the inclination to interfere.

Applying the Law

In your workbook write down what changes you could make in order to apply this Law to your daily life. For example … accept others' choices, offer help rather than impose it.

Law of Patience

1. It is said that patience is a virtue. What circumstances try your patience most?
2. What adjustments can you make to deal with this?

When you lose patience it is often due to a desire to control events or the speed at which they take place. There is a desire to be in the driving seat and there is a thought that you know that where you are going is for the best.

Be calm and relaxed, allowing events to unfold in their own time. This will be the right time. It is about trusting that there is a right time for everything and that all will be well. Be in the present without rushing into the future.

Allow others to develop at their own pace. Accept them and show love even if you disagree with their words and actions. Be loving and patient with yourself. Be aware of your actions and look at how you could do things better or differently but do not treat yourself harshly. Life is a learning process for all.

Be patient as the lessons unfold so that you do not miss the opportunities for learning and progressing. When you feel things are not going as you'd like, instead of becoming frustrated and impatient stop and go into the stillness.

You will then find that peaceful centre within and you will be able to resume tasks trusting that everything is taking place as it should at the right time and in the right way.

Patience is waiting. Patience is holding back. Patience is not jumping to conclusions. Patience is assembling the facts before doing or saying anything. Patience is giving someone the time to explain the whole story from their point of view.

Patience requires you to be calm, not to give in to your egotistical emotions. Patience requires you to see the whole picture. Patience is yet another manifestation of unconditional love. Patience is understanding. Patience is knowing. Patience is a demonstration of your spiritual progress.

Adopting an attitude of patience allows you to remain in control of your thoughts and actions. A patient approach will prevent situations from escalating into something that is not particularly nice for anyone. A patient approach will take the heat out of inflamed circumstances. Being patient shows you are knowing and understanding.

Being patient is a recognition that others have their lessons to learn from the situation. Patience brings calmness and patience is its own reward.

Applying the Law
In your workbook write down what changes you could make in order to apply this Law to your daily life. For example … be aware of my body becoming tense, remain calm and in self-control, realise everything will happen when it is meant to.

Law of Praise

1. Are you fulsome in your praise of self and others? What stops you?
2. When writing your journal remember to praise yourself for things well done. Read it over and check that you haven't just listed negative qualities and experiences.

Always be willing to praise others for something well done. It is good to let them know how you feel as this gives them motivation to do even better. Do not be jealous of the success of others. Rejoice with them and encourage them along their path.

If you feel praise is not due for whatever reason keep criticism to yourself and stay silent sending out only thoughts of love. Keep a record of your own actions and do not simply criticise yourself but praise yourself when you feel you have dealt with issues in a spiritual way.

When you sit in meditation remember to send out praise and thanks to all who assist you. Praise shows you appreciate others. Be liberal with your praise and be open to receiving praise back.

When you have received praise haven't you felt special? Didn't it give you a boost? It would be exactly the same for anyone who receives praise. Praise means you have done something particularly well.

We all strive to do our best and sometimes it works out that way and we get praised. We feel a glow of contentment. It travels right through to our inner self. We should always look for the best in others and we should let them know that we have found it. Those steps along the path become easier with the praise of others ringing in our ears.

Don't look for the negative, don't be critical. These are destructive forces and can do so much harm. Indeed seek out the positive. It is always there. Even the darkest night has lights. Give praise and watch the negative dispel. Watch the confidence grow. Be slow to criticise, but quick to praise.

Applying the Law

In your workbook write down what changes you could make in order to apply this Law to your daily life. For example ... realise what praise means to others, look for what is good more often rather than for what could be better, never hesitate to say "well done" when it is merited.

Meditation Suggestion

Visualise a group of wise beings discussing Acceptance / Non Judgment. As you approach them they invite you to sit down and listen. Take note of what they are saying. What can you learn from them? Thank them for allowing you to be there. Record what you learned in your workbook.

CHAPTER TEN

BALANCE

As above, so below. As within, so without.

Balance creates stability for all things. Allow all viewpoints without feeling you must defend your own. Do not let anyone tell you what your journey will be or what it must contain. Neither let anyone tell you what your reality is.

Law of Relativity

1. *When was the last time you were satisfied with something you did or achieved?*
   - *How did you know you were satisfied?*
   - *What feelings did you have that were different?*
2. *Think of a past difficult situation and write down something positive that came out of it.*
3. *Is there a current situation you find difficult but could give thanks for the experience?*

This law enables you to experience your positive qualities of love, joy and light. In order to understand fully what these are you have to experience the opposite for comparison.

Do not therefore complain when you go through what seems to be low times when there are experiences you would rather not endure. Endure all these and allow the experiences to enable you to appreciate the good qualities and experiences.

When you are faced with danger and fear is upon you you can then learn to trust the Universe to care for you. Without this experience how would you know you had the quality of trust? When faced with adversity you can fight back or you can invoke these higher qualities of love and forgiveness.

Be grateful for the experiences you encounter. Do not condemn them for you have chosen them for your spiritual growth. By being grateful for them you will bring out the qualities that will benefit you and others.

Look at the good and the bad, the happy and the sad. Remember you are looking at the Divine as God is all and all is God. Be grateful for what you do not like as it enables you to show your God like qualities.

Every thing is a gift and the most precious of gifts do not always come in the most expensive of wrapping.

Greetings. You have asked for guidance on this Law. All things are relative. Without relationship there is no knowledge. Without knowledge there is no wisdom. But in relativity what is the defining point? In scientific terms there are scales and measurements. How else can you measure temperature for instance. You can accurately measure with instruments but the answer is always relative.

In regard to spiritual matters the defining point is you. Where do you want to go? How would you like things to be? But you cannot use scales and measurements with any accuracy. You have to consider everything in relation to everything else. How do you know you are satisfied? How do you know you are fulfilled?

You can only tell from comparing with other incidents. You can only tell from past experiences. You can only tell from making comparisons. Your situation is relative. As you journey on your spiritual path you only know if you are progressing or not by comparing with past situations. Relativity.

You make informed decisions about your future by reviewing past situations. Relativity. There always has to be a thing, an event, a situation to compare with, for you to know where you are, how you feel. If you have nothing to compare against, then you cannot make a judgment.

The Spiritual Laws are not difficult my friend, but they need to be studied, and we are here to help you. With this Law it's as simple as it sounds. Your situation, although changing constantly, only changes because of relativity.

When you stop comparing you stop making movement. You seek growth but how will you know when you have achieved any?

Applying the Law

In your workbook write down what changes you could make in order to apply this Law to your daily life. For example ... do not look on the surface -- search for the good in everything, acknowledge the bad so that I know good, look on every experience as a learning opportunity.

Law of Polarity

1. *Recall a time when you made a fairly important decision.*
   - *What led you to that decision?*
   - *What were the alternatives?*
   - *Why did they not "measure up"?*
2. *What can you do to stay balanced in difficult situations?*

In everyday speech you talk about things being poles apart. They are so totally different they seem to be completely unconnected and yet everything in the Universe is connected.

You refer to day and night, heat and cold, male and female. Without the experience of each item in the pair you cannot gain knowledge and experience of what they really are. How can you fully know heat if you have never felt cold.

By experiencing all these aspects you can begin to know who you really are. When faced with difficult situations you learn to love and trust as you strive towards the light.

Seek out the good in all things. There is a need to find balance at all times e.g. there are good qualities which are perceived to be male and good qualities which are perceived to belong to females.

There is no purpose in rejecting one or the other. Strive to take on qualities from both aspects. Remember all things have a purpose and are there for your growth and experience.

Accept whatever comes to you and you will find the scales of life will always balance.

This is the Lady Nada. You have asked for guidance on the Law of Polarity. This is a Law of Extremes, and also a Law of Balance. It is not possible to define the middle ground, the middle path, the middle anything without reference to the extremes.

How do you know "warm" if you don't know "hot" and "cold"? Again how do you define the extremes without reference? How can you know "hot" if you don't know "cold"? One defines the other and both define the middle.

The Law of Polarity exists to show us the full range we can experience. Love and Hate. Rich and Poor. Dark and Light. It is up to each one of us, through the experience of the extremes, to determine how we shall live in relation to them.

How close to a pole will we choose? Life is a series of choices and Polarity defines that it will always be so. For every decision we make there is always an alternative. It is a question of experiencing each aspect and making a choice.

Without polarity there would be nothing to choose.

Applying the Law
In your workbook write down what changes you could make in order to apply this Law to your daily life. For example ... find more balance in thoughts -- do not go from one extreme to the other, look for alternatives and consider them before making a decision.

Law of Gender

1. List your qualities, both positive and negative. Now assign a gender to them. What does this tell you? Do you need to lessen some and have more of others to be balanced? Which ones?

There are qualities and attributes which are often associated with male or female. These qualities are sometimes perceived as good and sometimes seen as not desirable. They are seen as opposites but it is important for males and females to find balance in the qualities they have.

It depends on the circumstances involved and how you react as to whether a quality is being used in the right way. It is good to be loving and caring but a mother who shows this towards her child would become totally different towards someone who attacked her child.

It is the intention that is important. It is important to have the wisdom to find balance to know when it is right to display particular qualities. There is no place for extremes. It is important for children and even young animals to be with both parents so that they can see all qualities and hopefully find balance and wisdom within themselves.

The Law of Gender is about balance. There needs to be male and female. Even in a male person there are female traits and the result brings a balance and harmony. Too much of one or too little of the other results in an extreme.

Extremes by their very nature are at the edge, far from the balance point. Extremes of one sort will balance out with the extremes of the other sort, but ideally each person should have elements of each gender and be close to the midpoint.

There will be variations on either side of the midpoint but in general the bulk of the population will be found round it. This brings a balance to society, a balance to nature.

We should each strive to ensure that we maintain our position close to the balance point. The further we are removed from it, the greater is the certainty that we will not see the complete picture.

Look closely at yourself and ask where you stand in relation to the balance point. What qualities do you have to develop to get closer to it? Work hard to achieve the balance point. From here you can see all things.

Applying the Law
In your workbook write down what changes you could make in order to apply this Law to your daily life. For example ... examine my qualities regularly to see what is missing and develop accordingly, be more centred within myself at all times.

Law of Correspondence

1. How do you know when you are in balance? Do you need to experience the extremes?
2. Have you been through a stressful situation which resulted in ill health? What were the circumstances?
3. Have you received anger from someone and given it back, or vice versa? How could you have acted differently?

It is important to remember that you are body, mind and spirit. These are not separate and unconnected. To be in balance, health and harmony these three bodies have to be in balance with each other. If one is out of line then equilibrium cannot exist.

You are in a physical body but you will not achieve much if you ignore the existence of your other levels. Everything you do or think has repercussions on all levels. Be aware of all your thoughts and actions, remembering there will always be a reaction.

Being quiet and still assists in bringing balance to all levels. Reach up to your Higher Self in these quiet moments and the inner guidance will assist in bringing harmony at all levels.

As well as operating from different levels with these levels affecting each other, you are connected to every other organism. Remember the Law of Divine Oneness. You will then realise that your thoughts and actions do not only have repercussions for you on your various levels but affect all other life.

You cannot live in isolation. All is part of you and you are part of all. Feel all parts of yourself connected and you will feel connected to the Universe.

Connect within and you will connect without.

Greetings my child, this is Kwan Yin. You have asked for guidance on this Law. Basically and simply it states that everything in the Universe is connected. Only through this universal connection can there be balance. It's what gives you direction.

There can be no right without left, no up without down. If you have too much someone else has too little. There is enough for everyone if we would only recognise and accept it. Some struggle to survive, some have it easy. The Law of Correspondence asks you to seek out that balance, to achieve it, to help others achieve it.

Every thought you have, every deed and every action you take sends an energy across the Universe. It is like throwing a stone into a pool -- there is a ripple created and it travels outwards and would do so infinitely, and that ripple sways the vegetation growing in the pool, the creatures living in the pool are affected by it. The stone hitting the water can be detected a large distance away.

So you see everything is connected at the simplest and deepest level. Everyone is affected by everything and vice versa. We all give out energy and we all react to it. Correspondence is about achieving balance, harmony: when everything corresponds we will be in balance.

Applying the Law
In your workbook write down what changes you could make in order to apply this Law to your daily life. For example ... deal with issues as they arise, pay more attention to my body so that I know when there is an imbalance, monitor thoughts.

Meditation Suggestion

- Visualise a pendulum at rest. It is in the central or balanced position.
- Now watch as it is moved to one extreme and released.
- Watch as the pendulum swings to the other extreme -- it has to pass through the balanced position to get there.
- Continue to watch as it swings back, always going through the balanced position.
- As it slows down it begins to ease towards the central point, never quite reaching the extremes again, but always going through the balanced position.
- The pendulum passes through the balanced position more times than any other point.
- As you watch the pendulum slow down and seeking to return to the balanced point, realise that you too are letting go of all the negativity that drags you away from the balanced position.
- Together you and the pendulum reach a balance.

CHAPTER ELEVEN

GRACE

Grace releases Karma. Grace allows a person to receive that which will benefit their highest good the most. Grace allows one person to send another healing, to do soul work and not suffer the consequences of Karma, or interfere with the receiver's soul plan. Grace is working at a higher vibration.

Law of Grace

1. What are the qualities of gracefulness?
2. Go into the stillness and send love and forgiveness to anyone you have hurt in the past. You have to be able to demonstrate this -- words aren't enough. Working from the heart will bring a release from Karmic debt.
3. When was the last time you treated someone the way you would like to be treated?

Love yourself and love all others in order to bring in Grace. Continually examine your thoughts and actions. Praise yourself for work well done and look carefully at things you could have done differently. Were there words or deeds which could have been more loving? Do not condemn yourself or others but use the past to learn and progress in the future.

Send love and healing to past events and to those whom you have hurt or who have hurt you. Be prepared to forgive and move on, releasing yourself and others from the past. Whatever you do, consider others as well as yourself.

Whatever you ask for, ask that it is for the highest good of all involved. Be aware that all are connected at a spiritual level and that by loving yourself and others unconditionally you are bringing grace to yourself and to those with whom you are involved.

Grace is the quality of balance. The expression of serenity. An act of being in full control. You talk of grace and beauty, of grace and balance, of grace and poise. You describe some movements as graceful. What makes them such? It is the control that makes it so. It is the ease with which it is done that makes it so.

Grace is associated with what are seen to be the better things -- awkward movements are not considered graceful! Grace is that quality of inner control, of care, of love. It is hard to maintain that graceful poise if you are angry or upset.

When you allow yourself to become angry or upset you are losing control of your emotions. You are going out of balance. By calming down you regain your poise, your grace. Best results are always obtained when you remain calm and relaxed. This is what you should aim for.

Take time each day to relax, to still the body and the mind. Find that inner peace and you will find outer peace. You will also find grace. Give out unconditional love, let it flow freely, and you will see grace in action.

Grace. Balance. Control. Moderation. Calmness. Be gracious to all.

Applying the Law
In your workbook write down what changes you could make in order to apply this Law to your daily life. For example ... remain calm and relaxed in all situations, give praise where it is merited -- even to myself, be quicker to forgive.

Law of Forgiveness

1. *Are there any events in your past that you still hold on to?*
   - *Why can't you let them go?*
2. *Do you have any negative ideas around forgiveness? (sign of weakness, for example.)*
   - *Can you identify something in the past or present to forgive and how can you show you mean it?*

You cannot progress if you are tied to the past by feelings of hurt and resentment. You are focussed backwards instead of forwards and you are locked into situations and relationships which you need to break clear from to allow yourself and others freedom to move on in your own ways.

If you say you have forgiven someone you must really mean it and not expect anything of the other person. Because you forgive them doesn't mean their attitudes or behaviour will change. You have to be prepared for a time when you will need to forgive them again for the same thing. That is unconditional love --- not trying to change others, not having expectations of others but accepting whatever circumstances you are presented with.

If you do not set standards for others to achieve or behaviours which you would like them to display, you will be loving them without conditions and there will be no need for forgiveness as you will not be judging them against your standards. By letting events wash over you and moving on, you will not just be loving others but you will be acting in your own best interests as well.

Forgiveness is an expression of unconditional love. Forgiveness means you have not judged. It means you have not condemned. Forgiveness means you have accepted another's right to free will, to express themselves as they see fit.

The action or deed or words that you forgive through unconditional love may not be in accord with your beliefs, but you are recognising that others are free to form their own beliefs, no matter how different.

There is nothing to fear in forgiving -- it is more a sign of strength than of weakness. It can often take courage to forgive, especially when you feel hurt deep inside. Do not be tempted to hold back on forgiveness, for you are only creating problems for yourself. It is better to forgive, forget and move on.

Free will is the greatest gift you possess. Recognise it in others also. Forgiveness is such a recognition. Bear no grudges, hold no animosity -- discharge them to the Universe and make progress. Unconditional love, freely expressed will bring spiritual rewards.

Applying the Law
In your workbook write down what changes you could make in order to apply this Law to your daily life. For example ... do not hang on to things -- let them wash over me, realise that I cause hurt and upset. Do not deny others their free will, recognise that I am only responsible for my actions.

Meditation Suggestion
- Surround yourself with people who need your forgiveness and also those from whom you require forgiveness.
- Be aware of everyone, including yourself, sending and receiving forgiveness.
- Feel a release from the past and the freedom to move forward in love.

Further suggestions for Meditation

Meeting your Higher Self

- Find a place where you won't be disturbed. Sit or lie down, get into a comfortable position and close your eyes. Relax.
- Tune into your body and get a feeling of what it is like to let go. Be aware of how pleasant it feels when tension floats out of your body.
- Imagine you are walking along a path at the bottom of a grassy slope. What can you see, hear and feel as you follow the path up the slope?
- You stop for a moment to absorb the peace and tranquillity. As you do so you hear the gurgle of a stream and decide to leave the path to walk to the stream.
- In the distance, beside some trees, is a pond from which the stream flows and you decide to walk towards it.
- You reach the pond, sit down beside it and a feeling of great peace spreads through your body. You glance into the pond, and see your reflection.
- As you focus on your reflection you become aware of a shining light within your entire body also reflected in the water and realise that this is your Higher Self. This is the real you: the beautiful part of you which you often forget about. This is the part of you that knows all your needs, all your thoughts, and what is right for you.
- Acknowledge it. If you need an answer, advice, guidance or healing then ask your Higher Self to assist you. Take a few moments to be with your Higher Self and perhaps you will receive an answer in the form of an image, word, phrase, feeling or symbol. Thank your Higher Self for being there.
- Now it is time to leave the pond. As you leave you lose sight of your reflection, but you know your Higher Self is always with you, waiting to be asked to help at any time.
- Slowly come back to the room and become aware of where you are. In your own time open your eyes and have a stretch before getting up slowly

Greeting the Day
(This is best done outside)

Remember, if you are in doubt about making any of the movements suggested, then do not do so.

- Select a piece of music that is gentle, but uplifting, for example "Morning Has Broken".
- As the music plays, gently move your arms to and fro
- Sway with the music
- Move your joints as much as you are able to, but do it in a gentle fashion
- What sounds can you hear as you do this activity?
- How do you feel?
- As the music comes to an end greet the day with joy, love and anticipation.

Living the Laws

Be still and be silent
when guidance you seek.
Be honest, be kind
in the words that you speak.
Be thankful, be joyful
for all you've been given,
And when you feel hurt
make sure you've forgiven.
Be trusting, have faith
when troubles appear.
Have hope and have courage
to let go of fear.
Acceptance and patience
will help you see through
What seems like a tunnel
with no light in view.
When others have troubles
show compassion and care.
Judge not, but be generous,
remembering to share.
Know you're abundant
with all that you need.
Your kind actions and thoughts
are the right way to lead.
Be creative and active
in the tasks that you do,
And what you give out
will come back to you.
All life is one,
if this you can see,
You'll know how important
it is to just "Be".

The Pyramid

In can be helpful to view spiritual growth as a pyramid, with the base being equivalent to our physical existence with no awareness of other levels, and the point of the pyramid our ultimate spiritual goal, where we wish to be, with all bodies in balance and harmony. You may wish to visualise levels within the pyramid, depicting advancement along the way.

The bottom of the pyramid represents the life of one who lives totally in the physical. There may be an awareness of other levels but there is absorption with the problems of existing on the earth.

Everyday issues are of paramount importance and one seeks to resolve them by physical means, which means that peace can never be achieved. This is where physical therapies can have an influence and start to bring about awareness on other levels. As the physical body calms down and the mind is given a chance to lessen its activities some insights can take place. With determination progress can take place, but unfortunately that progress is often short-lived.

When problems become intense and ill-health results this may be a time when one seeks out healing. This, too, has a valuable place and can be the beginning of a long spiritual path to enlightenment.

Sometimes people expect miracles without any effort on their own parts and, if results are not forthcoming, will quickly reject the healing and move back down the pyramid. Those who are ready to move on realise the importance of the emotional and mental levels and begin to reach a deeper understanding of those levels.

Change does not come about overnight, but there is a real desire to gain understanding of these levels. This may come from activities such as reading, or attending workshops to find out how others have moved along their pathways.

There is knowledge gained and one learns the value of being in control of thoughts and emotions. This can be a time of great change and outlook as there is a measure of success in controlling one's experiences. However the journey requires more and more effort and the rate of progress can level out.

There can also be difficulties as a result of conflicting views gained from other people's thinking and beliefs. Well meaning teachers can put forward their ideas as the only right ones and can be very dogmatic. They may truly believe their ways are of the highest level spiritually, but they have become closed. They will ultimately fail to make further progress as they have shut out the possibility that there are ways to develop further. Whilst they have put considerable effort into their development and have shared their progress with others, they have stunted further progress by shutting out truth and by not keeping an open mind.

Those who become followers of these teachers also stagnate as they are relying on others instead of seeking truth for themselves. There are therefore many people who practise spiritual techniques and attempt to live a spiritual existence and that is good. However those who realise that they have to do the work for themselves and have the determination to keep moving forwards are the ones who will reach the peak of the pyramid.

As the top of the pyramid is reached all bodies -- physical, mental, emotional and spiritual -- are coming together and balance is in sight.

It's a long learning process and there has to be determination not to let setbacks prevent further achievements. Others can assist and a listening ear can be an asset. However it is only the individual who can do the work needed.

Those who bring greater balance and harmony into their lives are those who practise meditation and seek guidance from their Higher Selves and Beings of Light. They know guidance is available if requested. They know that every event, every experience is an opportunity for growth. They are grateful for all their experiences and look for the values they bring. They are aware that learning is an ongoing process, and keep an open mind with a willingness to change when need be.

That point at the top can never be achieved unless there is balance in every moment. This means "being" in every moment. The Bible says "Be still and know that I am God". Just "be" and you will realise that God is within you.

Putting the spiritual Laws into practice daily, monitoring your progress, being grateful for every experience, accepting whatever comes to you, realising the power within you to create your experiences and to change your thoughts and emotions will bring about "being" in a spiritual sense. Others will learn from you by your example and not by your dogma. By all means share your experiences -- that is service -- but don't forget to just "be" and to allow others to do likewise in whatever fashion they choose.

It isn't easy, particularly in the beginning, but results are achievable and when that state of being is achieved one realises how easy it was compared to going around in turmoil at the base of the pyramid.

16 steps to Living the Laws

1. Write down your intention to Live the Laws. State your commitment.

2. Take each day at a time and decide to live the Laws to the best of your ability. Each day's success is a stepping stone along the journey. Welcome each day when you rise and be joyful. Perhaps play some inspiring music such as "Morning Has Broken" to uplift you.

3. Be gentle with yourself, learning from your reactions, positive and negative. You may find it helpful to set aside a time of day to update your journal: this will assist you in using it wisely as a tool for progress.

4. Acknowledge the power within yourself and do not give it to others. Allow them to be themselves.

5. When difficulties or challenges arise welcome them for what they bring you. Ask for help and guidance. Look to the Spiritual Laws for answers. The Law of Unconditional Love will be a good starting point. Writing down the problem may be the first step towards a solution.

6. When faced with adversity see others as an extension of yourself. See them as Angels, Teachers, Guides who have been sent to give you experiences to grow Spiritually and display your Divine qualities.

7. Make everything you do a meditation, even when doing tasks you would prefer not to do. Using affirmations can help.

8. Take time each day for at least two quiet periods for relaxation / meditation. Fill your mind with positive thoughts and affirmations.

9. Collect poems, quotes from books, articles which inspire you and keep them in a folder for reference. Include anything you write yourself.

10. Surround yourself with things you find beautiful to uplift you such as flowers, candles, pictures. Be with nature.

11. Read over the Laws each morning. Make a small copy to carry with you in your wallet or pocket for easy reference throughout the day.

12. Know it's alright for things to be as they are. Know there is a purpose in all things even although you can't see the whole picture.

13. View everything as a blessing. Remember the wise man knows he is rich but he who loses his spiritual connection is always poor. Give thanks.

14. Avoid self pity and blaming others.

15. Pay attention to diet, sleep and exercise.

16. In daily life be aware when you have negative thoughts or attitudes. Turn then into positives and your feelings and emotions will change.

In Closing

We hope that, by having worked your way through this book, you are finding it easier to incorporate the Laws into your life, and not just having a knowledge of them without actually *being* them. This, we feel, is the key: to BE the Laws.

Whatever you have gained from this, be it small or large, we ask you to share with others. If you can find a group of like-minded people with whom to share ideas on the Laws and develop thoughts, processes and being, we urge you to join them.

We would appreciate any feedback you may have, any ideas you have regarding the Laws, and how you found the book as a learning guide. You can contact us by e-mail at wellwithin@hotmail.com. We are also happy to keep details of any groups who would welcome new members and would be grateful to be sent details that can be passed on. We will be arranging a series of workshops in the London area and would like to hear from anyone interested. We would also be delighted to come and lead a workshop in your area so long as there are sufficient numbers to justify this. Details can be obtained on our website www.wellwithin.freeserve.co.uk.

Every day brings each and every one of us new experiences and opportunities to "be" the Laws. If you have anything you want to share with us please do so. We all learn from each other. We each perceive the world according to our reality and it is wonderful to be able to share another's reality in a spiritual manner. Sharing is being of service, which, in turn, is an essential part of being on a spiritual pathway. We all have to walk our own pathway and we are faced with differing circumstances. What we have in common is our Divine Oneness and the Spiritual Laws which apply to all circumstances.

The Laws provide answers to all questions. Whenever we experience a situation and have doubts to how to react we should look to the Laws for guidance. The answer is there.

In keeping your journal be honest with yourself, for you will make no headway otherwise. Please don't give up on your journal now that you have worked your way through this guide. We urge you to make it an ongoing activity.

The more you apply the Laws, the more you will "be" the Laws, the more you will trust in the Universe and everything will work out for you. Look to nature for inspiration and upliftment, ask for guidance in your meditations: trust and you will be taken care of.

Living the Spiritual Laws means a life with less stress which, in turn, means better health.

When we go against the Laws we fight a losing battle. We cease to go with the flow thinking we (ie our ego) knows best. Each day can be a battle, not just against the outside world, but against ourselves as our physical body struggles to cope. We fear, we anger, we lose faith, we imagine negativity in the present and future and mull over difficulties of the past.

The fight / flight syndrome dominates our bodies when our minds are allowed to run riot. The fight / flight is intended to prepare us for fighting or running away but although this enabled our ancestors to cope with stressors we generally do not have similar stressful situations. Our stresses tend to be ongoing, relationship issues, work difficulties, financial problems. Nevertheless the body still responds to stress eg blood pressure rises, muscles tense, breathing gets faster. These changes can become our "norm" as problems stay with us and are not resolved.

Stress is not a modern phenomenon, it has been with mankind throughout history. What is different today is how we deal with it. The fight / flight syndrome was designed to kick in to get us prepared for a dangerous situation, and kicked out again when it had passed. Today it still kicks in when we are facing a stressful situation. However we tend not to deal with these properly or completely and so the syndrome never really gets a chance to kick out. The result is that we are pumped up all the time and that does us no good at all.

We have to let go. We have to let the stress out somehow. If we do not do it "voluntarily" it will release itself in any way it can -- anger, emotional outbursts, even illness. Be in control. Release your stress safely.

By trusting there is a purpose in all things, by being grateful for what we have instead of longing for what we do not need, by looking beyond the surface and seeing the good in all, by understanding we are all connected at a higher level, by showing unconditional love to others and ourselves and compassion for all life we can live in harmony and allow our bodies to find equilibrium. A peaceful mind creates a peaceful physical body with all the systems in balance. We can live each day as it comes, be in the present, be healthy in body and mind and realise that if we struggle less in stormy waters we will float and stay alive.

This book was written as a guideline for helping release that stress, to show you that there is a way. We haven't said it was an easy way, although we have said it is not the only way. We do not claim to be perfect having adopted these principles: no one is. However we do our best to follow them in our lives and we have noticed an appreciable difference. Our lives are better, we feel better, we are abundant. We do not need to compete with anyone for anything. We have learned to trust and we have been rewarded.

We know that every happening brings a message, and we look for it, even in what seems at first to be a bad experience. Many times over the past five years we have been in situations that were fraught, but, using the Spiritual Laws for inspiration we came through them, better, fitter, happier.

One of the first lessons we learned was to stop asking "Why is this happening to me?" and instead ask "What is this telling me?" This will help you to seek out the positive aspects in difficult situations. It is a good place for you to start too.

If you can do this then you will have started the Self-Healing process. Whatever you are hoping to achieve has to come from within. You must believe in it. You must want to do it. You need to start by healing yourself, otherwise you will not travel far on your new pathway. You need to know where you are now and where it is you are trying to reach. Having defined the beginning and end points you can then set yourself goals and targets that are achievable, but to do so you must get yourself "fit for travel". Take a good look at your situation and make a note of what you do not like about it, what it is about your current situation that you do not like and want to change. Then list out what you need to do in order to get yourself into a position to undertake your journey.

Hopefully the questions we have asked at the beginning of each Law will have helped you to make certain observations about yourself and your relationships. Hopefully, too, in asking you how you could apply the Laws in your daily life will have given further insights. Use these answers to determine how you will move forward.

Take time to go into the quiet. Do not be afraid to go within. Ask your Higher Self for help and guidance -- you will be answered. The more often you go within, the more confident you will become.

We have said that self love is important, and it is. So too is it important that you self heal: be fit in body, mind and spirit for the way ahead.

APPENDIX 1 -- Affirmation Writing

An affirmation is a positive statement which goes beyond the critical conscious mind and into the subconscious mind where it becomes part of our belief system. The subconscious mind is like a sponge which soaks up and stores information without reasoning. It will help if you link into your Higher Self when writing your affirmations to find out what you really need.

Throughout our lives our subconscious mind has often been negatively programmed by other people's faulty beliefs. Repeating affirmations fills the subconscious mind with positive thoughts.

It is important to generate positive thoughts. Thought is energy and positive thoughts attract positive outcomes and negative thoughts attract negative outcomes. For example if you think you are going to do badly in an exam you are more likely to fail. If you feel confident when you go into an interview you are more likely to be successful. Remember affirmations can be used for all sorts of situations.

The following guidelines should assist you in formulating your affirmations.

1. Get a pen and paper ready as it is important to write down your affirmations. This helps you clarify what you really want.

2. Your affirmation must be something you really want, not something that someone else thinks is right for you. It has to be something that will appeal to your emotions, something that will give you positive outcomes and satisfaction.

3. Keep your affirmation realistic. Make it something that is possible to achieve.

4. Make your affirmation positive. For example: "I am a confident person" rather than "I do not lack confidence".

5. Write it in the present tense so that when you say it, it is as though it has already happened. eg. I am healthy and energetic.

6. Make sure you write it in the first person eg. I deserve love and respect.

7. Keep each affirmation fairly short.

8. During relaxation periods each day repeat each affirmation slowly to yourself several times and if possible visualise yourself doing what it is you want to do or being the way you want to be. Visualisation helps to reinforce the positive thought in the subconscious mind.

9. Say your affirmations rhythmically and confidently. You may wish to record them on tape.

10. It is also helpful to write your affirmations on cards and put them up in prominent places in the house to remind yourself of them.

11. Drawing or painting what you desire and putting it on the wall will make your affirmation more powerful.

APPENDIX 2

Affirmations

- **Morning**

- **Evening**

- **Higher Self**

Morning Affirmation

I affirm that if I go through this new day with the right attitude, the right beliefs, the right outlook all will be well.

I will meet all situations, all individuals with a positive, loving attitude, knowing that nothing comes about by chance but as a gift from the Universe to enable me to learn and take in more light.

I affirm that if I remain in contact with my Higher Self I will receive guidance and direction when required.

I will allow my consciousness to rise up and not down. I will allow love to flow instead of fear and frustration. I will allow thanks to be given instead of the 'why me' attitude. This will show I trust that all things have a positive purpose and that I trust the Universe to protect and guide me.

I affirm my intention to look for the good in everything, knowing that I may have to dig deep to find it. However, I acknowledge that although I will not be able to see all parts of the picture there is nothing missing at a Higher Level.

I am therefore committed to looking forward to what this day brings, to looking for the positive aspects, the teachings it brings and to asking for help when I feel the need.

I will accept myself and others without judging. If, at the end of the day I feel I could have done better I will simply note this and look forward to tomorrow when I can put my new learnings into practice.

Evening Affirmation

I affirm that the experiences, encounters, emotions and events I have undergone today were exactly right for me in every way.

I affirm that if any experiences, encounters, emotions or events which I would have liked to occur did not happen, then this was also exactly right for me in every way.

I acknowledge that the Universe allows everything to happen in the right way and at the right time.

This allows me to experience trust, peace of mind and an inner knowing that all will be well.

I acknowledge that whatever occurred today happened for a reason and gave me a learning experience. As I look back at today's experiences I will endeavour to learn from whatever has occurred and to learn from my reactions. I will not dwell on mistakes but know that today's lessons were given to enable me to grow and evolve. It is up to me to use these situations to grow spiritually.

As I note the lessons the Universe has given me I will give thanks, accept whatever has occurred, sleep peacefully, knowing that the Universe does not make mistakes.

I therefore send love and healing to all events, all people that have been part of my experiences today and ask that any negativity that has emanated from me on whatever level is transmuted into love and light.

Higher Self Affirmation

I have the power within myself to enable me to be the way I want to be, to achieve what is right for me, to feel the way I want to feel and to find peace and health.

All I have to do is let go and tune into my Higher Self and acknowledge that Divine spark within me and all others.

I allow my Higher Self to guide me, heal me, empower me, fill me with light and love which can radiate to others.

These spiritual qualities are for sharing and as I let go of them that well within me will be replenished: for as I give so will I receive, and that ingoing and outgoing flow has no beginning and no end.

I acknowledge responsibility for my feelings, thoughts, actions and if I continually connect to the Source within me these will be loving and pure and the truth that abides within me will manifest without.

As I let in the light I open up as a bud grows and opens in the sunlight and the beauty and light are a guide for others, helping them to connect to the same Source of which they are part.

I promise to give myself the time and space to allow my Higher Self to communicate and by doing this I will continue to progress along the spiritual path I have chosen to pursue.

APPENDIX 3

Journal

Date	Event	How it went / reaction	Lesson(s) to learn
14 Dec 2001	A meeting I was due to attend was called off at the last minute.	I was annoyed that those concerned did not give me more notice.	To remain calm and trust that everything happens in the right way at the right time.
23 Jan 2002	Decided to give a donation to the first person / organisation asking for money and to do so without making judgments.	Gave loose change to street beggar.	1. Felt I had made a good attempt at implementing several Laws eg Charity, Acceptance. 2. Need to do this more often

Living the Spiritual Laws

Index

A

abilities · 22, 30, 51
abundance · 9, 40, 58, 66, 70, 76, 77
Acceptance · vi, 82, 109, 125
action · 13, 16, 17, 18, 19, 24, 33, 47, 49, 72, 77, 98, 103, 105
affirmation · 28, 76, 119, 120
afraid · 37, 46, 51
anger · 9, 18, 22, 73, 97
angry · 12, 50, 102, 103
attachment · 65, 70
attitude · 24, 25, 36, 41, 50, 74, 85, 122
attraction · 9, 29
awareness · 28, 36, 67, 107, 110

B

balance · 13, 26, 93, 94, 95, 96, 97, 98, 99, 102, 103, 110, 111, 112
beauty · 12, 30, 102, 124
blame · 13, 24, 28, 34, 36

C

cause · 15, 18, 19, 44, 74, 105
change · 12, 16, 17, 24, 25, 26, 28, 31, 36, 44, 46, 52, 55, 82, 104, 110, 111, 112, 125
choice · 52, 54, 82, 94
coincidence · 58, 63
compassion · 80, 81, 109
compensation · 66
connection · 12, 40, 42, 58, 98, 114
consequences · 18, 24, 34, 54, 82, 101
control · 18, 24, 26, 27, 28, 29, 36, 54, 59, 79, 82, 84, 85, 102, 103, 110
Correspondence · vi, 18, 97, 98
courage · 42, 43, 49, 105, 109
create · 12, 16, 19, 22, 28, 29, 30, 31, 33, 54, 71, 76, 112
creation · 12, 13
creativity · 30, 31
Creativity · v, 30, 31

D

dedication · 44
denial · 35, 36
desire · 46, 62, 84, 110, 120
despair · 42, 58, 60, 63
Divine · 12, 13, 58, 90, 97, 124

E

effect · 15, 18, 19, 25
ego · 35, 42, 51, 73
emotion · 49
energy · 13, 16, 22, 24, 25, 26, 60, 62, 63, 66, 68, 70, 71, 72, 77, 80, 98, 119
experiences · 13, 19, 24, 28, 30, 43, 46, 62, 71, 74, 82, 86, 90, 91, 111, 112, 113, 115, 123

F

faith · 57, 58, 59, 60, 61, 109
fear · 9, 11, 18, 34, 43, 52, 54, 62, 70, 72, 76, 90, 105, 109, 122
forgiveness · 19, 90, 102, 104, 105
free will · 50, 54, 55, 82, 83, 104, 105
freedom · 51, 52, 83, 104, 105

G

gift · 47, 52, 54, 66, 68, 70, 72, 74, 90, 105, 122
goal · 11, 63, 110
goals · 35, 37, 44, 50, 83
growth · 11, 16, 36, 54, 58, 74, 77, 82, 90, 91, 93, 110, 111
guidance · 7, 8, 34, 42, 44, 58, 60, 66, 74, 91, 93, 97, 98, 109, 111, 113, 115, 116, 122

U

unconditional love · 9, 52, 53, 62, 68, 71,
72, 74, 80, 83, 85, 103, 104, 105

V

visualise · 16, 29, 110, 120

W

weakness · 49, 104, 105
wisdom · 31, 46, 70, 91, 95